# TOWARDS A NEW THEATRE

## HAMLET

*GHOST*. I am thy father's spirit ;
    Doom'd for a certain term to walk the night,
And for the day confined to fast in fires,
Till the foul crimes done in my days of nature
Are burnt and purged away.   But that I am forbid
To tell the secrets of my prison-house,
I could a tale unfold whose lightest word
Would harrow up thy soul, freeze thy young blood,
Make thy two eyes, like stars, start from their spheres,
Thy knotted and combined locks to part
And each particular hair to stand on end
Like quills upon the fretful porpentine :
But this eternal blazon must not be
To ears of flesh and blood.   List, list, O list !
If ever thou didst thy dear father love—
    *Hamlet*. O God !
    *Ghost*. Revenge his foul and most unnatural murder.

HAMLET

1907

# TOWARDS A NEW THEATRE FORTY DESIGNS FOR STAGE SCENES WITH CRITICAL NOTES BY THE INVENTOR EDWARD GORDON CRAIG

PUBLISHED 1969 BY BENJAMIN BLOM, INC. NEW YORK

TO

# THE ITALIANS

IN RESPECT, AFFECTION, AND GRATITUDE;

TO THEIR OLD AND THEIR NEW ACTORS,

EVER THE BEST IN EUROPE,

THE DESIGNS IN THIS BOOK

*ARE DEDICATED*

First Published 1913
Reissued 1969 by
Benjamin Blom, Inc., Bronx, New York 10452

Library of Congress Catalog Card Number 68-56531

Printed in the United States of America

" If there be no great love
   in the beginning,
Yet Heaven may decrease it
   upon better acquaintance."
           MUCH ADO ABOUT NOTHING.

" The poet's eye, in a fine frenzy rolling,
Doth glance from heaven to earth, from earth to heaven,
And, as imagination bodies forth
The forms of things unknown, the poet's pen
Turns them to shapes, and gives to airy nothing,
A local habitation and a name."
           A MIDSUMMER NIGHT'S DREAM.

# FOREWORD

## ON TRUTH AND ERROR

"THE truth has always need of being repeated, because error is ceaselessly and repeatedly preached to us, and not only by some isolated voices, but by the crowd. In the newspapers, encyclopædias, in the schools and the universities, everywhere error holds the first rank; it is at its ease with the majority, who charge themselves with its defence."

GOETHE'S *Conversations with Eckermann*, 1822–1832.

# A WORD OF ACKNOWLEDGMENT

WHEN a man starts to acknowledge his debts, he is beginning his biography. I think no one has ever paid his debts—hardly found time even to acknowledge them all. As to the artist, he is up to his neck in debts, and that without owing any money. He is equally in debt to people and things. If everyone is not his master, nearly every*thing* is. How many masters have I had for a short time? How many assistants also? And all these have helped me so much in my work. Omitting to speak of nature, for nature is always ready to help you, and expects no acknowledgment, there is one master above all that I wish I had learned from earlier—Leonardo da Vinci. All the others walk on easier paths, take shorter cuts, and are ready with too clever or too many charming suggestions. He alone seems to me to be a great master ; not because he has painted the Last Supper and other great paintings, not because he erected great statues, and foreshadowed almost all the wonders of modern life, but because he seemed to know more things and to know them rightly, and to know more about human nature and know it more rightly, and because in all his work he is calmer than other modern artists. It is for this reason I wish I had earlier known and studied from him. As it is, I wish to acknowledge my debt to at least a hundred people. To begin with, I acknowledge my debts to the limelight men of the Lyceum Theatre, and to Rembrandt ; to Ruskin, to William Blake, and to Fra Angelico ; to Alexandre Dumas and to Henry Irving ; to Yeats, to Whistler, to Pryde, Max Beerbohm, Nicholson, and to Beardsley ; to Tiepolo, to Guardi, to Crawhall, Hugo, and to Piranesi ; to Vitruvius, to Whitman, to Andreini, Ganassa, and Martinelli ; to Gherardi, Delsarte, Otway, and Vecellio ; to my boy Teddy, to Raphael, and the Martinettis ; to Nietzsche, Walter Pater, E. K. Chambers, Skeat, and to Roget ; and last but certainly not least, to my father and mother.

But some of this acknowledgment applies only to this book. When you are tired of this book I have other doors to open, through which only a very few of those I have mentioned consent to pass with me. You are not to imagine that the work shown here represents more than my work as scenic designer between the years 1900 and 1910.

"Thus bad begins and worse " (*who knows*) " remains behind."

*Note.*—I wish to acknowledge the kindness of the present owners of several of these designs for letting me reproduce them here, and to thank Messrs. J. M. Dent & Sons, and in particular Mr. Hugh Dent, for the cordial way in which they have collaborated with me in the production of this book.

# CONTENTS

# CONTENTS

# LIST OF PLATES

# LIST OF PLATES

# TOWARDS A NEW THEATRE

## I

IT seems there is still very much to explain about the Theatre,[1] and the Art of the Theatre, before the world will understand rightly.

The danger of pointing in a new direction, even towards a familiar object, is very great. It is even greater where the object is strange to us. Everyone cries out "Where, where?" and is content when his eye alights upon the very first object that it chances upon. The difficulty he finds is to see far enough, and then, at that distance, to see in perfect detail.

If I point, for instance, to a mountain at a great distance from us, a child, sitting on the grass, will look up to see the tall grasses in front of his nose, and what he hears me say about the distance he will apply to the tops of these grasses. A woman standing by me, instead of looking in the direction to which I point, will probably look at me pointing. A man will probably look as far as he can. It is a thousand to one that his eye will be caught by something a hundred yards off, or even a thousand yards off, or it may be that a bird springing up from the bushes and floating off will catch his eye, and all interest in the mountain will be gone. It may be that he will take a castle on a hill to be the mountain; or there may be some who, looking as far as they can, searching the horizon, will finally deny that any such mountain exists.

It is a mountain that I am pointing towards—a high place; that mountain is the Theatre. If it were something else, I would call it something else. As yet I know no other name for it. Let it then remain the Theatre, and please believe me when I tell you it is A MOUNTAIN. It is not a hill, nor group of hills, nor any mirage of hills—it is the largest mountain I have seen. No one has yet been able

---

[1] THEATRE.—According to Professor Skeat, a French word, derived from Latin; the Latin word from Greek. Middle French, *theatre*; Cotgrave's Dictionary, ed. 1660. Derived from the Latin *Theatrum*, derived from the Greek θέατρον, a place for seeing shows, derived from the Greek θεάομαι, I see. Compare θέα, a sight; see Prellwitz.

Note: Not a word about it being a place for *hearing 30,000 words babbled* out in two hours.

to scale its heights, because there is something evidently very strange about this mountain. Had it been easily accessible, it would have been climbed long ago. Now, tell me, don't you consider there is something very strange about this? People have wandered about its base for thousands of years, and no one has ever gone to the top, and many there are who refuse to believe that it has a top; but as I have seen the top, I wish flatly to contradict the many. I have seen the top from the distance; Fuji is not crowned more beautifully.

It is towards that mountain that I am attracted, and since I began to move in its direction, I find that I have come a little nearer to it than I was when I set out twenty-five years ago.

On my journey I have come across some curious people. I have met some who went past me and back to the place from whence I started, and who in passing told me they were going in the direction of that mountain. Some I met with backs turned to it who assured me they had just been there; "it wasn't very much to see after all." They had a disappointed look on their faces. Others there were who described it to me, saying, "It is just six thousand and fifty-two and a half feet high; it is an extinct volcano, and the middle class inhabit the summit. The climate is very dry; the trade in cinders is very brisk." These people have been looking at the wrong mountain. Others who profess to have come from there say that it is ruled by ladies—and the rest of their story is too ridiculous to repeat.

Now this is all very well for use as paragraphs in the Press, but it isn't the truth. Nobody has scaled those heights; nobody's report concerning those heights is correct. Everybody lies about it, for everybody is talking of something else.

I do not lie about it. I don't tell you that I have discovered the place: I tell you I am moving towards it. I do not tell you I am moving towards a new temple, for that also would be a lie. I am moving towards a new Theatre, and this book is one of my contributions towards a new Theatre. All that I have put in the book now lies behind me. I found it in the level plains, not even on the rising ground, far less in the heights, and therefore you must not get too excited about the little discoveries—for now the larger and finally the great discoveries await us.

There will be many theatres before the Theatre comes, just as there are many plateaus in the mountain. It is for this reason that I call this book "Towards *a* New Theatre" instead of "Towards *the* New Theatre." If I were to speak of *the* new Theatre, some of you would be sure to think I spoke of the new theatre which is to be opened in three or four years, and as I write in the English language, you would be sure to think I meant the new English theatre, and to say to yourselves, "The English theatre is *the* theatre." One of the first things the English have to do is to get out of their heads a belief that the theatre exists in England only, and to remember that there is a theatre in France, a theatre in Germany, theatres in Russia, Italy, Spain, Hungary, Sweden, Norway, Denmark, and even in Switzerland and Finland, and then don't let them think that they have thought of all the theatres, for there is a theatre beyond the Caucasus, a theatre in the East, and there is even a theatre in America and in Africa.

To which of them is my contribution made? To none of them, for there is still another new Theatre being founded, and it is to that Theatre that I offer the contents of this book. It is not offered as you offer food; it is given purely as a warning. There is not a thing in this book that can be of any practical "use" to you whatever except as a warning, and for your own sakes, and for the sake of the ideal Theatre, don't seize upon this book in the hope of extracting from it something[1] which can be put instantly into practical use in the belief that it will bring you nearer to our ideal—it is more likely to bring you £10,000 a year if well worked, but that, in my opinion, would be highly unpractical—for £10,000 is hardly worth more than a song—and one should learn how to refuse such little sums if one is serious about the large ideals connected with the Art.

As I have said before, what is here is what I have passed. Look at it if you like. Pay it a certain amount of reverence by fearing it—and, I hope, enjoy it.

There is a particular kind of fool in the theatre who amiably asks, "Why shouldn't I make use of an idea which is a good idea?" and there is surely

---

[1] One is reminded of a famous and gleeful little satire on the art of extracting, by some unknown master which runs as follows :

> "Little Jack Horner sat in a corner
> Eating a Christmas Pie,
> He put in his thumb and pulled out a Plum
> And said 'What a good boy am *I*.'"

somebody who will say, pointing to one of the pictures in this book, "Now that is a really good idea. What objection is there to my stealing it?" and they may even go so far—though it is very unlikely—as to add, "Of course I will publicly acknowledge, in programme and elsewhere, the source from which I have taken it." This particular kind of fool does not see that by acting in this way he is weakening himself and the theatre which he is supposed to be serving with some spirit. That is why I ask you and him to fear the influence of my book. I suggest to you both that if in this book you find certain ideas which you feel you could apply with success to your new production, take Punch's advice— "Don't." If, on the other hand, you want to develop your talents as a scene designer, not for immediate profit, but so as to become a better worker, then my book is at your service. But skip the public parade—avoid the danger of showing off what is not yet yours.

An idea is only of value because of the life *which gives it birth*, and nothing but original vibration can ever give life to it again. Even then, when recreating it, it will come out a little different, and it will not therefore be the same idea ; so that when an Autolycus of the modern European theatre takes one of my ideas and thinks that he puts it into practice, he has done nothing of the kind, for there is a great difference between a reflection in a mirror and the thing reflected. The difference is all a matter of life, and it is so contemptible too to copy an idea when by a little activity of soul and body you can give birth to an idea yourself and so add life to life—and if you have no ideas, don't be ashamed of admitting it.

What we do not want is these dead ideas, these copied things, and every-one should protest against the obvious hoax being practised month after month in the theatre of England of passing off unoriginal ideas as though they were original. One of the faults I find with English criticism is, that even the best critics enthusiastically chase after some copied idea, ignorant of the fact of the existence of the original, or, if conscious of it, criticising the copy in the same terms as they would use towards the original.[1]

---

[1] This seems to me to be a little fault which might easily be prevented if English critics were *given the opportunity* to study what is being done in the other cities of the British Isles and in the other cities on the Continent. The English critic should be sent by the rich English journals to Paris, to Berlin, to Krakau and to Budapest. The public deserves to know what is being done in these and other places. Who had heard of Strindberg, for instance, until he died—and had it not been for Mr. William Archer, who so often went to Norway, who in England would have heard of Ibsen? Then, just lately, were we informed by

# TOWARDS A NEW THEATRE

Finally, this book represents my preliminary efforts in *one division* of a phase of theatrical art which I have passed through. As I have written in my book "On the Art of the Theatre," the artist of the Theatre of the future will create his masterpieces out of action, scene, and voice. That was in 1905, and the future to which I referred is still before us, and therefore anybody, who can go into the matter more thoroughly than I did, is still free to alter that and to show that it can be created out of something different . . . something finer, simpler. My reason for mentioning it here, is to call your attention once more to something which some of you at times overlook when speaking of my work. That is to say, I am not concerned alone with what is called the "scenic" part of the art. I would like you to remember that I have clearly stated that action and voice are the other two parts which I am studying. Action and voice cannot be satisfactorily treated by means of the written word or diagrams, whereas scene to some extent can be so treated.

It is therefore the scenic division which comes into this book ; and as prelude to the pictures themselves, I have now something to say about stage scenery.

the journals about the revival of the art of improvisation under Hevesi in the theatres of Italy and Hungary ? Does anyone know about Wyspiansky and his school ? But who is there that does not know of the third-rate imitators of these people ? The London Press gets hysterical about third-rate imitators when it is the duty of the editors to see that we are given sound information about the origin of these imitations.

# II

ONCE upon a time, stage scenery was architecture. A little later it became imitation architecture; still later it became imitation artificial architecture. Then it lost its head, went quite mad, and has been in a lunatic asylum ever since. Some day, when my school comes into being, we will issue a book dealing with the historical facts of this case. I shall see to it that my scenic work receives justice—(I fear that very little of it will ever see salvation)—but here and now is not the time nor the place to pull it too much to pieces. I could do that probably more thoroughly than any of my critics do. My remarks apply to the designs (with eight exceptions) in this book. These thirty-two drawings represent work done between 1900 and 1910. That work is now part of my past, and although I can look back at it with interest, I have no very great sentimental affection for my work of yesterday just because it is mine. That it is not so entirely without sense or without taste doesn't in my opinion excuse the fact that it is not quite right as stage scenery. It will not bear comparison with the noblest scenery when the conditions of the stage were noblest. At the noblest period that we know of, there was little talk of "simplicity," and less talk of illusion, and the scene *painter* was utterly unknown. In those days they built their theatres for their dramas, not their dramas for and in their theatres. They played in the day-time, and with the sun streaming upon the actors and audience alike, and didn't indulge in what is called "lighting effects."[1] They didn't waste an enormous amount of time trying to get some false colour that would look true by artificial light. Neither did they paint their faces with magenta and yellow ochre so as to look as if they had just come from the country.

But they didn't abstain from doing these things to be more natural, but only so as to be truer. Now, it is very difficult for the ordinary reader to

---

[1] At Letchworth, in the autumn of the year 1912, I was fortunate enough to be present at a performance practically in the open air, where artificial light was banned. England is quite an ideal country for open-air and daylight performances. In the south of Europe it is uncomfortably hot—here in England it is cool; and the rain is always a natural legislator which prevents an exaggerated number of unnecessary festivals. Festivals are for the spring-time; one month is enough.

understand what one means by truer, and it is really hardly necessary for him to understand, so long as the stage artist understands. I never met one of them in England who could entirely understand, or if there are one or two, they have never let me into the secret of their existence. I wish they would, for this sort of work gets rather lonely after a time; but to be true in art is not to lie to yourself, and that is very difficult and very expensive. But it is no waste of time nor of life; it is a form of gambling where you bet on a certainty. There is the National Gallery opposite me as I write to bear witness to the truth of the statement, and there is Nelson too. Risk your life for the arts either of peace or war, and you cannot fail to win. But there must be no limitations; you must not think that to have talked about simplicity and beauty for a season, or made a speech before the Playgoers' Club in which you went against the taste of the day before yesterday, that you have risked anything more than the contempt of the angels; and I say this because I do not want you to think that I should disagree with any serious critic who would advise me to take all my designs and burn them up as being unworthy of the highest traditions of scenic art. For these designs, as I have said before, and indeed many times, in one place or another, are my efforts *in one division of a phase of theatrical art*—a phase through which I have passed. Compare them with the scenery of the Greeks, which is, I suppose, the oldest scenery we know anything about, and you will see how they suffer by the comparison. Compare them with the second noblest scenery for Drama, the scenery of the Christians, and they seem little better. Compare them with the third period, when men began to make imitation architecture for artificially-lighted theatres—that is, in the sixteenth century—and they seem fairly good. I think that they would have held their own on the stage against the designs by Peruzzi, Serlio, Palladio, and the others; I think they are much better than the rococo scenery of Bibiena, and I must say that I think they triumph over latter-day scenery. The question as to just where they triumph and where they are defeated I cannot go into now nor here, but I can tell you something of the several periods of stage scenery without bothering you with many dates or names.

When Drama went indoors, it died; and when Drama went indoors, its scenery went indoors too. You must have the sun on you to live, and Drama and Architecture must have the sun on them to live. Of course you may say that "hanging on" is "living," but it is practically being dead—alive. Drama was able to be out of doors and in the sun because, instead of being a nightly amusement, it was a rare festival. People have always spoken about it as being a religious festival, but perhaps it is a mistake nowadays to underline this, because the word "religious" to us means one thing and in the old days it meant another thing. How best to describe what it was in the old days? Probably if you were to stand in St. Mark's Square—or even in Trafalgar Square, for the matter of that—on a sunny day, and see a couple of hundred pigeons wheeling round the square, flapping their wings, enjoying themselves in their own god-like way, you would get the nearest idea to what a Greek festival was like. And have you ever noticed that the people in the square passed on and took no notice of such an event? No; you will find that even the dullest man in the street will stay and watch the performance. Just such a performance is being played in front of my window as I write. Over fifty or sixty people have stopped to watch it, and that without a single advertisement having been put up. There are many people who will tell you that the Greek drama attracted because of its display of human passions, because of its beautiful girls dancing (such people always imagine that beautiful girls danced in the Greek dramas), or because of some subtle intellectual force which held the audience in its grip, and so forth. But it was nothing of the kind. It was simply that the Greeks had captured many of the secrets of nature from the birds, from the trees, from the clouds, and were not afraid to put such simple secrets to a religious use. And the chief secret which they caught was a small part of the secret of movement. It was the movement of the chorus which moved the onlookers. It was the movement of the sun upon the architecture which moved the audience.

A later-day critic, speaking of a performance given in some open-air theatre in Italy, where the architecture was the only scenery employed, tells of the emotion created by the passage of the sun during the drama. He was unable to describe it exactly, and I think that very few people could do so either, and then only in a poem. But he spoke of how time seemed actually to be in motion. The movement was felt, but felt through seeing.[1]

After the Greek came the Christian theatre—that is to say, the Christian Church. The theme of their drama, if no more tragic than that of the Greeks, was perhaps gloomier. For scenery, architecture again was used, and we may

---

[1] Remember here the derivation of the word "theatre." See note on p. 1.

see what kind of stage they had by looking at photographs and drawings of the choirs and sanctuaries of all the early Christian churches. We see stages rising one above the other, the windows placed at certain angles to illumine the stages, the entrances so arranged that movements of single figures or groups are made significant. We see the seats for the musicians, we see the very places on which the chief performers (for we may call them performers) stood, in which direction they faced, and even what they did. All this is recorded. The drama they played is known as the Mass.[1] The main difference between this theatre and the theatre of the Greeks is that it was closed in, although daylight, and sunlight in particular, was still employed.

The people flocked to these religious theatres as bees to a hive. Not a word that was spoken could they understand, for all was in Latin, and yet they flocked. Could you guess why they went there? It cost them nothing but what they chose to give. Perhaps that was the reason. Anyway, do not let that worry us; let us keep to the scenery.

Against the architectural background were placed decorations of gold and jewels, silks, velvets, and other precious materials. I wonder if the people would have preferred these things if they had been made out of paste-board and tinsel? I wonder if the same excitement and reverence could have been awakened before a Cross of papier-mâché?

What made this wonderful theatre a failure after a few hundred years? Nothing but the exhibition of limbs in a circus. That was too much for the people. They couldn't resist it. One understands it, but one doesn't understand the nature of the rulers who were so mad as to put that before a not very grown-up Europe. As well might one take one's children to see "Scheherazade" as call the children of a nation away from so beautiful a drama as the Mass to see a lot of boys and girls dancing nude in a circus. For the people in Europe at that time were just as innocent as our children are. You may say that it was time that they should grow up; but look how they have grown up. You will say that I am not quite exact, and that there is as much stupidity in children as there is divinity in them. I agree with you. But if there is an equal amount of both—and I think that this is true—why make a point of encouraging the

---

1 "The central and most solemn rite of the Christian worship was the Mass, an essentially dramatic commemoration of one of the most critical moments in the life of the Founder."—E. K. Chambers, *The Mediæval Stage*, vol. ii. bk. iii. p. 3.

stupidity? You will say that the religious theatre had grown dull, and that the other thing was a relief. So like Europe, that "relief"; the whole of modern deterioration seems to be based on that word "relief." In the old days, when a champion prize-fighter was getting the worst of it, and was at his last gasp, there was no talk of relief. I believe that one of the methods employed was to seize hold of a bradawl and plunge it into him. Now it is all relief. However, let us get back to the scenery, if you please.

After the Greek and Christian theatres had gone under, the first false theatre came into existence. The poets wrote elaborate and tedious dramas, and the scenery used for them was a kind of imitation architectural background. Palaces and even streets were fashioned or painted on cloths, and for a time the audience put up with it. These plays were performed in actual palaces, and as the people could not get a glimpse of them, they thought they would create a theatre of their own, and at the same time they set out to give the aristocracy a treat. Then the great Commedia dell'Arte arose.

As a background they took the houses and palaces of a street, not painted palaces, nor painted houses, but the real houses out in the street. Architecture again. Open air again. Sun again. And this theatre survived for about three hundred years. It gave birth to Shakespeare and to Molière, and the Shakespeare theatre is about the last theatre that flourished in the open air.

What numbers of books have been written about this Shakespearean theatre, as if it were an original idea, as if it were the first of its kind, as if never before had the open theatre been "given a chance," as if it were the beau ideal of that kind of thing. As a matter of fact, the Shakespearean theatre was the very last and the weakest breath of the open-air theatre. We should avoid anything like a return to the Shakespearean theatre, because it was built on the mere leavings of a former magnificence. I suppose there are thousands of books and articles written about this Shakespearean stage. How many books are there about the Commedia dell'Arte and its stage, about the Christian theatre and its stage, or about the Greek theatre and its stage? I have seen a few, but hardly any of them are adequate. As a background to his plays, Shakespeare had a nice little wooden cosy corner of a stage erected in a bear-pit, but his plays really belong to a much more magnificent open-air theatre than that. The poor wooden "O" which he regretted so much is made into a very pompous "O" to-day, and if we are to do Shakespeare justice on his own lines, we shall build him a theatre very different from that of the Globe, if also very different from that of Drury Lane.

After the Shakespeare stage passed away, the daylight was shut out for ever. Oil lamps, gas lamps, electric lamps, were turned on, and the scenery, instead of being architectural, became—pictorial scenery. You cannot call it picture, for picture is that which is concerned only with two dimensions, and were you to ask Leonardo da Vinci or Cezanne, I think that they would agree with me that scenery is not *picture*. Yet every day we get people speaking of scenery as if it were picture, and even painters have the temerity to enter the theatre and put on to the stage the result of their studies as painters. They are all descendants of Bibiena, and I hope they are proud of him. Nothing pleases them so much as the artifice of the modern theatre, and they "use" the stage, at the same time having a contempt for its tricks. I suppose that they like this so much because they know nothing about the beauty of the ancient theatre. I can only think of this as their excuse, but it brings us no nearer to a noble stage—it brings us no nearer to noble scenery. Many of my own scenes, of which there are forty in this book, in my opinion bring us very little nearer.

When I began working, there was no school for theatrical art, there was no one to tell me these things that I have told you; and it is only now, after many years' working, that I have seen the direction in which we are all going. And now I do not point back to the Greeks, I do not point back to the Christian Church, nor to any noble theatre that we have possessed, nor tell you to reconstruct these. I care not a scrap about the past, but only about the future; but what the finest in the past teaches us is exactly the same as the finest in the future, and to reach this old new ideal—perhaps even to surpass it in time—I go towards a new Theatre.

# ON A STAGE DECORATION BY BIBIENA

"OUR system of decoration was properly invented for the opera, to which it is also in reality best adapted. It has several unavoidable defects; others which certainly may be, but which seldom are, avoided.

"Among the inevitable defects I reckon the breaking of the lines in the side scenes from every point of view except one; the disproportion between the size of the player when he appears in the background and the objects as diminished in the perspective; the unfavourable lighting from below and behind; the contrast between the painted and the actual lights and shades; the impossibility of narrowing the stage at pleasure, so that the inside of a palace and a hut have the same length and breadth, &c.

"The errors which may be avoided are, want of simplicity and of great and reposing masses; overloading the scenery with superfluous and distracting objects either from the painter being desirous of showing his strength in perspective, or not knowing how otherwise to fill up the space; an architecture full of mannerism, often altogether unconnected, nay, even at variance with possibility, coloured in a motley manner which resembles no species of stone in the world.

"Most scene painters owe their success entirely to the spectators' ignorance of the art of design; I have often seen a whole pit enchanted with a decoration from which the eye of skill must have turned away with disgust, and in whose place a plain green wall would have been infinitely better. A vitiated taste for splendour of decoration and magnificence of dress has rendered the arrangement of the theatre a complicated and expensive business, whence it frequently happens that the main requisites, good pieces and good players, are considered as secondary matters; but this is an inconvenience which it is here unnecessary to mention."

A. W. SCHLEGEL.

And what Schlegel says here applies fairly well to this stage decoration by Bibiena. The design is a triumph of the artificial. If artificiality is what we

12

DESIGN FOR A SCENE BY GIOVANNI MARIA BIBIENA, 1625-1665

# ON A STAGE DECORATION BY BIBIENA

want in the theatre, then this is a triumphant design for the theatre. But artificiality is not what we want in the theatre. The artificial only falters and lisps, and that is only rather pretty when it is in its right place. Still, the artificial is not excluded from nature's scheme. But it is as unwise for us as artists to exaggerate one of the sillinesses of Nature as it is unwise to exaggerate her noble ways, omitting all the silly ones. If Nature is not to be looked at by the artist as she is, then away with eyes, ears, and everything else. You look at her like that, and then you write a story about her, omitting nothing, but flattering her in a most natural way. If you omit to flatter her, you might as well not have been born. She gives birth to you, and in that she flatters you, and the least you can do is to return the compliment.

13

"ENTER THE ARMY"

1900

# "ENTER THE ARMY"

THAT'S a stage direction, and *that's* a drama.

I sometimes live in Trafalgar Square, where all sorts of undramatic things go on all day long, but when I hear a band in the distance, and I see the troops coming along, I feel that although it is merely a regiment of men, it is dramatic. What you may say is, that it is theatrical. Strange, that troops marching so trimly should be called theatrical! Is the effect theatrical? I do not think so. I think the effect is dramatic. That the army may be General Booth's army, and that they are carrying his coffin to the grave, does not seem to me to make it more dramatic, but the fact that it is a body of men in uniform and that it is marching in unison, *that* seems to me very dramatic. If they were all divided and split up, in what way would they differ from the ordinary? In the entrance of the army we return to the old feeling that was in the entrance of the chorus in the Greek drama or the entrance of the choir in the medieval drama. The idea of the chorus may be old-fashioned to some people. Certainly the spirit of harmony and uniformity is not a very modern spirit, and, except in the army, or among the police, or in a cricket match, we seldom are aware of its presence. But in art, it seems to me entirely forgotten, and yet it is the one essential thing that should be remembered.

Well—"exit the army."

15

Mother from Ted.
1901

THE LIGHTS OF LONDON                    1901

# THE LIGHTS OF LONDON

THIS was one of my earliest designs. Previous to this, when I produced a play, I scrawled out rough designs with a blue pencil, and did not translate them into anything pictorial. If I had had a theatre in 1900, I should never have been forced to make these designs, and I should have preferred it had I always been enabled to work directly with the material which the theatre offers, rather than with the material which the draughtsman is given. The two things are, of course, entirely separate, and, had I not been born in a theatre, I should have made fantasies which could not possibly have been realised on the stage. As, however, I was, I was able, through my experience of the theatre, to make designs which can very nearly be perfectly materialised.

If you will look at them carefully you will see signs of this. I think you will very seldom see things here in perspective : avenues leading up to goodness knows where and which no one could walk on. I remember that when the curtain was down and I was on the stage during the *entr'actes*, I would often stroll up to what is called the " back cloth," and while the music was tinkling in the orchestra, and the people were being called on to the stage, I would gaze longingly at the mountains painted there, or the twisted high roads which led to the mountains, and I would fancy myself walking along them. Those were fancies in which I often indulged. As a young actor, and when dressed for the character I was to represent—in fact, when out of myself—I really think I used to believe that these back cloths were real. I remember a delightful cloth in " *Olivia* " painted by Hawes Craven, and another delightful one painted by the same artist for " *Ravenswood*." The first was an English landscape—Yorkshire hills and a delightful evening sky ; little cottages dotted about in the distance ; and I remember there was a large country-seat—I suppose it was meant to be Squire Thornhill's Manor House.

In the " *Ravenswood* " scene there were thousands of small trees growing on a slope covered with bluebells ; there were not just a few bluebells in patches, the slope was entirely covered with them.

17

# THE LIGHTS OF LONDON

I used to get quite near these back cloths, and I remember I always used to touch them. I would put my finger on Squire Thornhill's house, or on the large oak in the distance, or, with my two fingers, I would wander up some lane. Anyhow, my whole desire was to get into the picture, and I always regretted that I could not do so. It was for this reason, I suppose, that when I came to design scenes for myself I avoided putting any place in my picture which could *not* be travelled into actually by the actors.

Now if in the drama you have mention of a staircase which no one was ever able to ascend or descend, and if the dramatist wishes to show that nobody ever will be able to ascend that staircase, then there seems some sense in *painting* it instead of building it. But if steps are to be shown in some scene—let us say in "*Julius Cæsar*"—which not only fantasy but common sense would people with many figures, then it is preposterous to paint those steps—they must be built; for if you only paint them, and no one ever passes up or down them, you suggest to the spectator that there was something very eccentric about Rome on that particular afternoon. Is not this true?[1]

So you will see this rule running right through my designs. There is not a spot in them which could not be walked upon and lived in. Where I have introduced a pyramid, as in the design for "Cæsar and Cleopatra," on page 55, I have put it so far off that in nature no one would see the figures upon it. It is at such a distance that our imagination alone could people it—and our fancy runs up and down it with ease.

This first design in my book was made for "*The Lights of London*." I left out all the lights of London which other scene-painters had put in, and I included the one light they had always left out. To be natural nowadays is to be eccentric.

---

[1] There was a garden scene in a certain production of "Twelfth Night" that I once saw which contained a long flight of green grass steps, and it gave no sense of illusion to the spectator, for no one ever went up more than six or ten out of one hundred steps. Then they all turned off sharply to the right or the left—six or ten were real steps, the rest all painted. Champfleury, writing of stage scenery, says: "Be false—but false from first to last, and you will be true." Like most paradoxes, there is truth in this. But what is better to remember is that we must always be true to Nature—and can always be true to her——when we understand her. Painted steps, windows, and other such details, which have to be used, or could be used, are unnatural and therefore out of place.

18

THE MASQUE OF LONDON

1901

# THE MASQUE OF LONDON

THIS also is for a play the scene of which is laid in London. In 1901 I wrote the scenario for a "Masque of London," and this was one of the scenes designed for that Masque. There is another scene in this volume for this London Masque, supposed to be Wapping Old Stairs. In the original drawing, from which this reproduction was made, all is not entirely grey. There are three or four tiny pieces of very pale blue seen through the grey clouds, and these prevent the spectator from feeling hopelessly miserable—these and the white church in the middle keep the tragic place reasonably gay.

The little white churches which you see over the roofs of London, starting out of the sea of grey in the most surprisingly virginal manner, how beautiful they are! At night, too, they become even more beautiful. I have never understood how it was that scene painters could never give us the majesty and poetry of London when asked to design scenes for modern plays. I suppose it is that the play-writers wanted nothing majestic. The nearest approach I have seen to a fine interpretation of London on the stage was at the Surrey Theatre, in a lurid melodrama, called, I think, "Her Second Time on Earth." There was a view of the London streets by night from the top of a roof, and the painter, whoever he was, had evidently got the right idea. There seemed to be at least twenty thousand lights, set in great curves, but this is the only example of a grand London scene I can remember. It came near suggesting the magnificent and beautiful thing London is. Oh, for a writer who should spring up in our midst and compose a great dramatic poem which alone can give expression to the glory of the place we live in! I am at his service on the day he arrives.

These mean-spirited interpreters of the capital of England sicken me with their narrowness of vision. The two-inch marionettes which they create, calling them Mrs. this and Mr. the other—what have they to do with London? Dickens gets nearer to the real beings, but Dickens is too comfortable, and Dickens has, unfortunately, to be dramatised by an amiable assistant before his characters can be brought on to the stage.

19

HENRY V—THE TENTS

1901

# HENRY V—THE TENTS

THIS scene represents the trenches surrounding the English camp. The king's tent is seen in the background, and the fence stretching across the middle of the scene is for the comedians. They enter from behind, climbing up on to the fence and speaking while perched up there like sparrows on telegraph wires, changing their positions just as sparrows flit from one side to the other. I think comedians would be able to put this scene to good use. Comedians generally can ferret out the ideas of a scene and make use of them. If only tragedians could do so, all would be well. The only men who can play tragedy as it was meant to be played are now in the music-halls or at the Gaiety.

If Mr. G. P. Huntley had not given so much time to the lighter forms of tragedy, he could by now be terrorising the English public in the heavier forms of comedy. The only serious performance I saw in London last year was a light entertainment by Mr. G. P. Huntley at a music hall. Even Grasso, the Sicilian tragedian, who was playing on the same evening, was not more grave.

Well, I suppose we shall have to look to our comedians for tragedy. Mr. Pellissier as Cardinal Wolsey was certainly a most terrifying figure, in a tragic little skit I once saw in London.

"THE ARRIVAL"                                                              1901

# "THE ARRIVAL"

THIS is for no particular play, but it is for what I believe to be true drama. The name explains the drama. The first picture in this volume ("Enter the Army") is a stage direction; so is "The Arrival" a kind of stage direction. It tells us of something which is being done, and not of something which is being said, and the fact that we do not know who is arriving and why they are arriving, or what they will look like when they appear, makes it, to my mind, dramatic. "And," you will say, "unsatisfying." That depends. That depends if you are more interested in the end than in the middle or the beginning. It seems to me that the longer one postpones the end, the more exciting life must be. To open the golden doors and find nothing but great glittering stars, to have to admit to Bill "that there ain't no heaven," seems to me a stupid thing to hasten. Provided that you do not open the doors, you never know, and that is heaven. Maeterlinck, of course, maintains that to know the room one sits in is to find it heaven, but that won't do.

I feel that dramas should never tell you anything. I don't mean that you should never hear any words spoken, although that would be a great blessing, but the things done, the ambitions awakened, should never be finished—they should always be a mystery; and mystery no longer exists the moment things finish; mystery dies when you touch the soul of things or see the soul quite clearly. Then, what nonsense we talk when we speak about the mystery of this play or that play, when these plays are perhaps rather mysterious, but entirely comprehensible. You wish that I would be a little more comprehensible. If I wished to be, I should say what I said ten years ago, "Give me a theatre," and then you shall be like blind Gloucester, and "see feelingly."

"*Lear.* Read.

"*Gloucester.* What, with this case of eyes?

"*Lear.* Oh, ho, are you there with me? No eyes in your head, nor no

23

money in your purse? Your eyes are in a heavy case, your purse in a light; yet you see how this world goes.

"*Gloucester*. I see it feelingly."

But I no longer want a theatre. We no longer need theatres. We need first to become masters of the art. Let us turn, then, to our studies with all the seriousness left in us after hundreds of years "*pretending*."

CINDERELLA

# CINDERELLA

THE design on the last page was dated 1901. This one is dated 1904. What could I have been doing in between those times, that there is no design of 1902-3 to put in this book?

I was designing on a stage, operas and plays and masques, and there was therefore less need to translate my full intentions on to paper. I have a great boxful of sketches and diagrams of this period on paper, but they are not for this book. They shall have a book to themselves. These designs were for " Dido and Æneas," " Acis and Galatea," " The Masque of Love," " Sword and Song," " The Vikings," " Much Ado about Nothing," and yet an old Scotch friend said to me the other day, with his fine biting accent : " Craig, you have only to show them what you can do on the stage of a theatre, and then you will get all the support you want. Begin in any simple little way," he said, " a little room somewhere, and you won't want any money to do it, everybody will work for you for nothing, and you will go on for several years, and then everyone will support you." I told him that the people who worked with me in the operas of " Dido and Æneas," " Acis and Galatea," and " The Masque of Love " all worked for nothing, about eighty of them, and for about eight months on each production. But that was when I was thirty, and before I understood that to ask for free help is to spoil the millionaires. All willingly contributed their time and energy to the task. Of course one could still go on asking people to contribute these, but I have made an important discovery since those days. The people whom I ask to work with me must have two particular qualities which are very unique ones. First, obedience ; second, enthusiastic loyalty. These two qualities they must all possess, or obtain or develop. Now if they succeed in the task to which I put them, that is the end of my demand from them ; but I am by no means going to sit down and see these people, who succeed where others fail, passed over and taken no notice of. They would, I have no doubt, work for me, as this friend of mine suggested, till kingdom come, if I were to call upon their loyalty and

25

their obedience. But once having found these two qualities in them, they shall have everything else; and could I find two thousand workers with but these two qualities, the theatre should have everything else, and then the nation should have the theatre. One really ought to explain a little what one means by enthusiastic loyalty and obedience, for these two things are so little understood nowadays. How best explain in a word? I think the whole idea is summed up in the word "family." One has heard of sons and daughters being obedient to their father. Some say that this obedience is the strength of a nation. Doubtless it is natural, pretty, and healthy. Two things are necessary—that the father shall know everything about the house, and that the sons shall not pretend to know anything until it comes to their turn to play the father, and that the daughters shall learn to despise cats.

Well, then.

THE MASQUE OF LONDON—WAPPING OLD STAIRS                    1904

# WAPPING OLD STAIRS

AT the time that I designed this, I was living in a little studio somewhere in the middle of London, and hating the very sight of man except on those days when I could afford to ride on a 'bus to Hampton Court. At this time I was writing a strange kind of mimo-drama, planning it out, designing all the scenes, and the movements; and it was called "Hunger." It was a fearful thing. I was asked to produce it in Berlin, but by that time I had escaped into a nice encouraging city, and I found that it was a little unfair. I think in that mimo-drama I had brought together all those wretched lazy yet "respectable" women who carry two thousand pounds around their necks and fruffle their skirts, and seem very detestable. I do not think I understood that they are not quite so detestable as they seem, but indeed I hated them so heartily at the time that I smeared them all over the pages. They were the reason why a whole family was done to death upon the stage in front of your eyes in this comic-tragic thing called "Hunger." There was a king in it, a great fat creature who was wheeled about in a chair like a large frog; he was a kind of money king, swollen through eating too many dinners at the Savoy. Not a real king, of course—a beast of a king—and I remember his entrance particularly pleased me. He was wheeled on, ready throned on an invalid's throne that seemed like a sea of cushions; those who propelled him were the chief gentlemen of the Court. Their progress was made in this manner: first four steps, and then everyone nearly fainted with fatigue—a fanning—a smelling of salts during a pause, silence, and a tiny, squeaky voice from the depths of the cushions calling for relief. Then another bold effort—four steps forward and another pause with the same play repeated. So at last they reached their destination. I do not think I shall have anything more to do with this drama until I can show the other half of the truth. The hunger of the poor was put down right enough, but the hunger of the rich had not been fairly treated. I daresay it is as tragic.

27

# WAPPING OLD STAIRS

At the same time I was preparing a second mimo-drama to be called "London," and the picture facing is one of the designs that I made. I never finished the drama, but I remember it began somewhere in Persia or Arabia. In a great hall, flooded with light, so that you couldn't see in what land you were, a philosopher and a poet were discovered meditating (as they meditate in the East—not at all like a brown study), and the poet was Blake's poet who saw *through* his eyes, and the philosopher saw *with* them. And the poet would not believe all the things which the philosopher was telling him of London, so he was taken out of Arabia, out of the sun, and landed at Wapping Old Stairs. There he was shown that London is the place to which all the dead souls of men are brought and placed in some wretched case, either that of a newspaper boy or a shoeblack, given some trade, some papers to sell, some boots to black, and sent along to his business. And I remember they all arrived in great barges down the brown Thames, and were shot out like sacks of coal and sent flying up those steps, their names or numbers being shouted out by some infernal spirit who stood ticking them off on a paper. There was another scene, and then I left it.

In this design, however, the two figures, or rather the first one, seems to be getting the best of the place. I do not suppose it is at all like the actual Wapping Old Stairs of to-day, but perhaps you will overlook that.

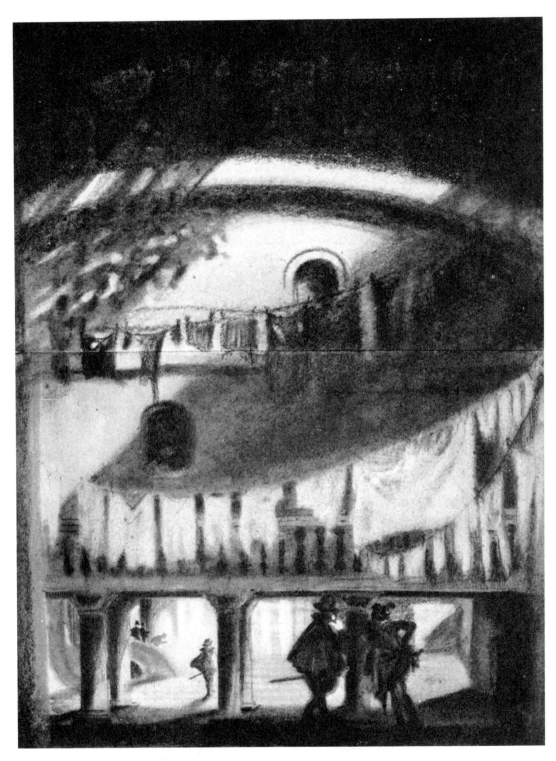

VENICE PRESERVED, ACT II.                                        1904

# VENICE PRESERVED

ONE of the designs I made for the scene where the conspirators meet in a little street in Venice. I would not propose such a scene for any theatre except one of a special form—that is to say, with the seats all on an inclined floor. How wonderful it is that one should speak of such a theatre as being a special one, and that every theatre in the world should not by this time have all its seats on such a floor! Germany was taught this by Richard Wagner, and has now, I suppose, at least thirty or forty such theatres, and every year there is a new one. What am I talking about? Why, at least ten new theatres are being built there every year. One sees so much in the papers about German ships which are being built, as if one defeated a nation simply through ships. Why, you can defeat them through the theatre—I don't mean by saying rude things about them on the stage, or by flattering ourselves and our own courage and our own ships on the stage, but I mean by building theatres which are ahead of the times, or at least up to date.

*WE ARE BUILDING THEATRES SIXTY OR SEVENTY YEARS BEHIND THE TIMES, AND IT IS NOT THE SHIPS THAT ARE GOING TO LOSE THE BATTLE WHEN THE DAY COMES, IT WILL BE THE THEATRES AND THOSE OTHER ANTIQUATED INSTITUTIONS.*

Worse than that. We are not even building old theatres. The other day I was in a garden city which is supposed to be, experimentally, rather ahead of the times. No one was to be found who would build a theatre for the young fellows who were working to create a theatre there, and who have been working to create a theatre there for a couple of years. If this had been a German garden city—and I believe Germans are beginning to build them—one of the first things which they would have put down as necessary, as essential to the life of the place, would have been a theatre, designed by one of the most go-ahead young architects, in which a different play would be performed every night—classical as well as modern plays—in which probably one thousand people could be seated, in which the most advanced of our dramatic writers, stage managers, scene painters, and the rest, would be given full opportunity to go ahead. And the extraordinary thing is that no one in England will believe it when an Englishman brings news from Germany of the great activity of the German theatre.

I suppose hardly any of you have read Otway's "Venice Preserved," but, as you can imagine, it is laid in Venice—a Venice built by Otway, who perhaps knew very little about it, and cared less, but who followed the fashion of the time, and employed Venice as a background for his drama of passion. Hugo von Hoffmansthal of Vienna had adapted more or less freely Otway's masterpiece for a German theatre director, and I was asked in 1904 to go over to Berlin and design the scenes and costumes for the tragedy and to superintend the production. I did this as well as I could under the conditions, and as an indication of the circumstances, I will give you an example of what I mean. I showed this picture, for the last scene but one, to the director, who formerly had been a literary critic, and who had only studied the theatre for a few years, and then not as an artist, but as a "literary gent." He looked at it with some suspicion. He then looked at me with more suspicion, and asked me where was the door. I said, "But there is no door." I said, "There is a way in and a way out." He said, "Yes, but I see no door handle nor lock. You cannot have a door without a handle." But again I repeated "There is no door. There is a way in and a way out." This very nearly sent him into a rage, but he changed and became quite calm again and pleased when I informed him that it was copied exactly line for line from an old Italian manuscript. I leave the reader to guess whether I had copied it or no. You see the trouble is, and always will be, that certain theatrical men in high places have no imagination. I did not want this nice old gentleman to imagine a door, but I wanted him through his imagination to see that no door was necessary, and I only succeeded when I assured him that it was a replica of an actuality. Now this good man was particularly unwise in making it impossible for me to consider any second piece with him by this unimaginative way of looking at things, for within three or four years he practically lost control over his patrons, who left his theatre and went over to the opposition theatre, which

VENICE PRESERVED, ACT IV.                                          1904

was managed by a friend of mine, and who had the—what shall one call it?—the *nous* to make use of my old ideas (so they said), and so fill his theatre to overflowing.

One has to say these things now and then, and it is easier to do so when no longer in competition with any managers or theatrical ventures whatever.

HAMLET, ACT I. SCENE 5

1904

# HAMLET

### ACT I.—SCENE 5

AS frontispiece to this book, I have another design for this same scene in Hamlet. One was made in 1904, the other in 1907. It shows you what I really think of the actor and of his powers. In the 1904 design, you see I have put him in a place where he can dominate with difficulty. In 1907 I put him in a place that would need a hero to dominate it.

Why put the actor in a Guignol Theatre?

Everyone calls him a puppet, and, by Roscius, if he is to be one, he shall be a superior puppet. He shall be as small as you like, the place shall tower above his little head, and yet he shall dominate it. His face shall go, nothing shall be left but his actions, and yet he shall dominate it. Movement shall be taken from him, and he shall be placed in so hopeless a situation that nothing but a mask shall be left him, and yet he shall dominate. But all this shall be done only at enormous self-sacrifice for the sake of the theatre. "But why sacrifice?" says somebody. Well, if it can be done in any other way, all the better, but it never has been done, and it seems that it never will be done. "Why?" you ask. Well, when you have answered all the questions the poet asks about the flower in the crannied wall you will be much wiser than ever I could be, and there will be no need to ask me. If there are no mysteries in life, then life is of absolutely no value; but every tiny thing is a great mystery, and every tiny thing should be treated as such.

So shall we develop ourselves and dominate the world and that much more difficult thing—ourselves. Then we shall indeed be ACTORS.

33

ELECTRA

1905

# ELECTRA

I HAVE never seen Electra acted, although I have seen the play done in a theatre. I saw it in Germany. My impression was that Electra was a little lady taking a little revenge with a lot of gusto. This impression was created because there was no beauty in the performance, and as no beauty, no Truth. "And what is Truth?" asks jesting Pilate. And Keats has answered him once and for all. Beauty is the complete, and even a touch of it here or there in a performance showing that the performer has perceived the complete is enough to show us that the performer feels like a true artist. If you are able to show that you have seen the complete completely, then you create a great work of art. This is not all said to prove anything in favour of or against the design here, but perhaps there is the faintest glimmer in it of something which may be called beauty. I no longer have the eyes to find it there, although it is one of the designs that I like best to keep. What really is the best definition of beauty? It cannot be that which throws spirit and matter out of harmony! You cannot take sides: the two things must be fused, before beauty can come near the place.

JULIUS CÆSAR, ACT II. SCENE 2                                    1905

# JULIUS CÆSAR

## ACT II.—SCENE 2

*Enter* CÆSAR, *in his night-gown*

*CÆSAR.* Nor heaven nor earth have been at peace to-night ;
Thrice hath Calphurnia in her sleep cried out,
"Help ho, they murder Cæsar !"    Who's within ?

*Enter* A SERVANT

*Servant.* My lord ?
*Cæsar.* Go bid the priests do present sacrifice,
And bring me their opinions of success.
*Servant.* I will, my lord.                                    [*Exit.*

*Enter* CALPHURNIA

*Cal.* What mean you, Cæsar ? think you to walk forth ?
You shall not stir out of your house to-day.
*Cæsar.* Cæsar shall forth ; the things that threatened me
Ne'er looked but on my back ; when they shall see
The face of Cæsar, they are vanished.
*Cal.* Cæsar, I never stood on ceremonies,
Yet now they fright me.    There is one within,
Besides the things that we have heard and seen,
Recounts most horrid sights seen by the watch.
A lioness hath whelpèd in the streets ;
And graves have yawned, and yielded up their dead ;
Fierce fiery warriors fought upon the clouds,
In ranks and squadrons and right form of war,

37

Which drizzled blood upon the Capitol ;
The noise of battle hurtled in the air,
Horses did neigh, and dying men did groan,
And ghosts did shriek and squeal about the streets.
Oh, Cæsar ! these things are beyond all use,
And I do fear them.
  *Cæsar.*                What can be avoided
Whose end is purposed by the mighty gods ?
Yet Cæsar shall go forth ; for these predictions
Are to the world in general as to Cæsar.
  *Cal.* When beggars die there are no comets seen ;
The heavens themselves blaze forth the death of princes.
  *Cæsar.* Cowards die many times before their death ;
The valiant never taste of death but once.
Of all the wonders that I yet have heard,
It seems to me most strange that men should fear ;
Seeing that death, a necessary end,
Will come when it will come.

THE PRINCESS IS STOLEN 1905

# THE PRINCESS IS STOLEN

THIS was an incident in a mimo-drama to have been called " The Life of a Princess," and this is one of her earliest adventures. I suppose the scene would do equally well for any other play that was romantic, and so I find it very difficult to say anything about it except that " Here it is."

THE STEPS I

1905

# THE STEPS I

## FIRST MOOD

I THINK it is Maeterlinck who pointed out to us that drama is not only that part of life which is concerned with the good and bad feelings of individuals, and that there is much drama in life without the assistance of murder, jealousy, and the other first passions. He then leads us up to a fountain or into a wood, or brings a stream upon us, makes a cock crow, and shows us how dramatic these things are. Of course, Shakespeare showed us all that a few centuries earlier, but there is much good and no harm in having repeated it. Still I think that he might have told us that there are two kinds of drama, and that they are very sharply divided. These two I would call the Drama of Speech and the Drama of Silence, and I think that his trees, his fountains, his streams, and the rest come under the heading of the Drama of Silence—that is to say, dramas where speech becomes paltry and inadequate. Very well, then, if we pursue this thought further, we find that there are many things other than works of Nature which enter into this Drama of Silence, and a very grand note in this Drama is struck by that noblest of all men's work, Architecture. There is something so human and so poignant to me in a great city at a time of the night when there are no people about and no sounds. It is dreadfully sad until you walk till six o'clock in the morning. Then it is very exciting. And among all the dreams that the architect has laid upon the earth, I know of no more lovely things than his flights of steps leading up and leading down, and of this feeling about architecture in my art I have often thought how one could give life (not a voice) to these places, using them to a dramatic end. When this desire came to me I was continually designing dramas wherein the place was architectural and lent itself to my desire. And so I began with a drama called "The Steps."

This is the first design, and there are three others. In each design, I show

# THE STEPS I

the same place, but the people who are cradled in it belong to each of its different moods. In the first it is light and gay, and three children are playing on it as you see the birds do on the back of a large hippopotamus lying asleep in an African river. What the children do I cannot tell you, although I have it written down somewhere. It is simply technical, and until seen it is valueless. But if you can hear in your mind's ear the little stamping sound which rabbits make, and can hear a rustle of tiny silver bells, you will have a glimpse of what I mean, and will be able to picture to yourself the queer quick little movements. Now on to the next one.

THE STEPS II                                                    1905

# THE STEPS II

## SECOND MOOD

YOU see that the steps have not changed, but they are, as it were, going to sleep, and at the very top of a flat and deep terrace we see many girls and boys jumping about like fireflies. And in the foreground, and farthest from them, I have made the earth respond to their movements.

The earth is made to dance.

THE STEPS III

1905

# THE STEPS III

## THIRD MOOD

SOMETHING a little older has come upon the steps. It is very late evening with them. The movement commences with the passing of a single figure—a man. He begins to trace his way through the maze which is defined upon the floor. He fails to reach the centre. Another figure appears at the top of the steps—a woman. He moves no longer, and she descends the steps slowly to join him. It does not seem to me very clear whether she ever does join him, but when designing it I had hoped that she might. Together they might once more commence to thread the maze. But although the man and woman interest me to some extent, it is the steps on which they move which move me. The figures dominate the steps for a time, but the steps are for all time. I believe that some day I shall get nearer to the secret of these things, and I may tell you that it is very exciting approaching such mysteries. If they were dead, how dull they would be, but they are trembling with a great life, more so than that of man—than that of woman.

THE STEPS, IV                                                    1905

# THE STEPS IV

## FOURTH MOOD

THE steps this time have to bear more weight. It is full night, and to commence with, I want you to cover with your hand the carved marks on the floor and to shut out from your eyes the curved fountains at the top of the steps. Imagine also the figure which is leaning there, placed over on the other side of the steps—that is to say, in the shadow. He is heavy with some unnecessary sorrow, for sorrow is always unnecessary, and you see him moving hither and thither upon this highway of the world. Soon he passes on to the position in which I have placed him. When he arrives there, his head is sunk upon his breast, and he remains immobile.

Then things commence to stir; at first ever so slowly, and then with increasing rapidity. Up above him you see the crest of a fountain rising like the rising moon when it is heavy in autumn. It rises and rises, now and then in a great throe, but more often regularly. Then a second fountain appears. Together they pour out their natures in silence. When these streams have risen to their full height, the last movement commences. Upon the ground is outlined in warm light the carved shapes of two large windows, and in the centre of one of these is the shadow of a man and a woman. The figure on the steps raises his head. The drama is finished.

47

# STUDY FOR MOVEMENT

HERE we see a man battling through a snowstorm, the movements of both snow and man being made actual. Now I wonder whether it would be better if we should have no snowstorm visualised, but only the man, making his symbolical gestures which should suggest to us a man fighting against the elements. In a way I suppose this would be better. Still I have some doubts; for, following that line of argument in its logical sequence, then, would it not be still more near to art if we had no man, but only movements of some intangible material which would suggest the movements which the soul of man makes battling against the soul of nature? Perhaps it would be even better to have nothing at all. If this is to be, then art, being almost at its last gasp, to-day we seem to be nearer perfection than we were even in the days of the great symbolical designers of India. But if we are to have the actual man going through actual gestures, why not have the actual scene going through its actual pantomime?

I don't know if anybody is really very interested in such questions; no one seems to be making any efforts to answer them one way or another. Let us turn over the page.

STUDY FOR MOVEMENT

1906

# CÆSAR AND CLEOPATRA

ALTHOUGH I really designed this and the following two scenes for myself, it may be more exactly said that I designed them for Professor Reinhardt. How many scenes I have not designed both for myself and Professor Reinhardt it would be difficult to say, but in 1905, he asked me for the fifth or sixth time to produce him a play, and of course, the moment anybody asks one to produce a play one gets excited. My son asks me to produce plays every now and then, and then I get really excited, and in the same way, I grew really excited with this suggestion of Professor Reinhardt's. I set to work, and in a couple of days had put down in colour eight or ten projects for the production. I remember I also made a model for the First Scene. One does these things when one is young—that is to say, on Monday or on Tuesday—but when one gets older, on Wednesday, one foolishly stops doing these things. For instance, someone suggested the other day in London that I should produce such and such a play. Now instead of rashly running to paper and pencil, and creating something which might interest me later, I said to myself : " These people are not serious. The thing will never take place." And so I have lost for myself a couple of days' excitement and some very nice designs. They are not serious, these people who invite artists to begin a work and then get frightened at their own request, but for all that I advise all young men to be rash. All contracts are fairly worthless in the theatrical world, and an invitation to collaborate in a work for the theatre equally valueless, but what is valuable is the hope which is inspired in you when some "important" person says : " Will you do this for me, Herr Jones, or Senor Smith ?" Of course you instantly say to yourself with a beating heart (for the artist's heart is always young and properly foolish) : " This is tremendous ; all my dreams as an artist will be realised. We shall all of us be flying soon." And you rush off and you make ten designs. That is on Monday, when you are young; and on Wednesday you become cautious because you find that the world is old, and one half of it a really very dreadful place—even more dreadful than you are yourself. Extraordinary !

49

CÆSAR AND CLEOPATRA, ACT I. SCENE I 1909

# CÆSAR AND CLEOPATRA

## ACT I.—SCENE 1

I HARDLY think that Mr. Bernard Shaw will like this design, but that is his own fault. He should have designed the scene for us. He wrote the play, he also wrote the stage directions in full, then why did he omit to design the scene and the costumes? If you meddle with the tools of a trade, it is best to master them—and for a dramatic writer to add stage directions to his written play, and to omit to show how those directions are to be carried out, is to tinker. In the Greek and Elizabethan drama you will find no stage directions.

I was asked to produce this play in Berlin, and the only thing I could do was to forget to read the author's stage directions, so that I might make sure of getting at the meaning of the play. And as I read the words, I wanted to omit these too, for the Scenario Scene seemed so excellent. When I had got the words out of my head I looked to see what was left of the First Scene, and I found this First Scene to be a great rat-trap in which figures were hurrying and scurrying to and fro like so many squeaking animals, one real figure standing out in a comic tragic mask—Ftatateeta. So you will see in my design no other individuals whom you can recognise, and only the figure in the centre rivets the attention.

CÆSAR AND CLEOPATRA, ACT I. SCENE 3          1906

# CÆSAR AND CLEOPATRA

ACT I.—SCENE 3

IF you have read the play, you will know this is the scene which culminates in Cæsar and Cleopatra being seated side by side on the throne, and she turns to him and asks him to point out to her where is Cæsar. I put the bars all round to keep out the mob and the soldiers, so that we have Cæsar and Cleopatra quite alone in the scene. And yet the actors say I never think of the leading actor and actress. They would be more exact to say that I sometimes let my eyes wander away from the centre of the stage. What the actors seem to forget is this, that plays are not made up entirely of the leading actor and actress, and although you may have them, as in this case, in the centre, and very much in the centre, there are other times when it is essential for the drama that the leading actor and actress shall be in a corner or under an extinguisher. That is what "star" actors will never admit. There must be times when they are absolutely extinguished, when they appear ridiculous, and not only ridiculous, but loathsome or pitiful; but the leading actor or actress always wants to be sympathetic and central. He wants to be loved the whole time from first to last, but he fails in achieving his purpose just because he forgets that love is not a thing made up of only one feeling, but is necessarily made up of every feeling. Therefore the leading actor is not really loved on the stage. For instance, in Macbeth you never really detest the man, and yet it is necessary to detest Macbeth before you can understand him thoroughly. You never feel that he is ridiculous—so ridiculous that you feel ashamed to sit in your seat; and yet if the actor were serious, even in his own work, leaving aside the drama as a whole, and shutting out the truth that the actor should make no personal appeal, if he were even as serious as this, then he would certainly do as I say, and would move every feeling in the audience both against him and for him. He possesses them from the start—he has no fear

53

# CÆSAR AND CLEOPATRA

that he will lose them.   Very well, then.   Play with them. Risk everything
with them.   Yes, you say, and empty the theatre of them.   Not at all.   In all
the past centuries the theatre has never been able to be emptied.   The Church
has tried to empty the theatre, the State has tried to empty the theatre ; everything
has tried, and everything has failed.   What, then, is all this nonsense that people
talk about the danger of running a theatre successfully, and especially the danger
of being an artist in the theatre ?   Does Giovanni Grasso empty the theatre ?   Did
Tomaso Salvini, Irving, Talma, Andreini, and Gherardi empty the theatres ?

.        .        .        .        .        .        .        .        .        .

I am very sorry that I have not talked about this design, but you see the
moment I think of the scene it makes me think of the actor.

CÆSAR AND CLEOPATRA, ACT I. SCENE 2                    1906

# CÆSAR AND CLEOPATRA

## ACT I.—SCENE 2

THIS is not at all like the Sphinx, as you probably know, but it is not unlike the Bernard Shaw Sphinx. As I have said in another book, when the stage manager sets to work to design a scene, he acts as interpreter, following the lead of the poet or the playwright; and this picture is a good example of what I mean. I know something of the sculptures of Egypt, and I know this —that it is light in tone, sharp cut, and as sharp in the moonlight as it is in the sunlight. It is the noblest of all art. So noble are these creations that I would never bring them on to a stage as they are. Like noble ghosts, they should be invisible. But here it was a matter of putting on a Socialistic Sphinx, and I put him down in less than thirty minutes. Instead of sharp precise lines, with virtue in every inch of them, the Socialistic Sphinx must be splodgy, restless, threatening. He must be hardly out of his tiger stage—one could almost write his " stage-tiger stage."

That little cat who looms so large in the First Act of the play will not be out of place crawling in and out of the wrinkles of this monster. I have only one request to make. Should you ever go to Egypt, take this drawing with you and compare this monster with the god at the foot of the Pyramids. Then I shall have " received satisfaction "—you will never look at my design again— no, nor think of " Cæsar and Cleopatra."

DIDO AND ÆNEAS, ACT III. SCENE 1                    1906

# DIDO AND ÆNEAS

THIS was designed for the opera six years after I had already once produced it. It is intended for the scene which precedes the last scene of all, in which there is a sailors' chorus—"Come away, fellow-sailors." When I presented the opera in 1900, with my friend Martin Shaw, I had only a plain blue background which has become dreadfully popular since then. Lights from above placed on a "bridge" which we built—a grey proscenium, such as many of the German theatres have used since 1904—a colour scheme—very little movement. This very little movement is a characteristic of the English temperament, and, being incomprehensible to other nations, is avoided by Germans, Russians, and French.

# DESIGN FOR AN ENTRANCE HALL OF A THEATRE

ONE of these days we shall get away from the gilt and the rococo and the inconvenient conveniences of modern theatre buildings. We shall argue about it a great deal before then, and we shall hear a lot of nonsense about what the public wants, and how it wants only stupid things, cheap things, and uncomfortable things, and this will go on for quite a number of years, but we shall come round to exactly what I say and what many of us feel, and we shall have our beautiful theatres, only they will be far more beautiful than any of us can picture. But it is quite likely that use will be made of this design before passing on to a more beautiful one. Here we have a stairway which leads from the first hall of the theatre into an open foyer, and so on through the doors at the back into the auditorium. It would do equally well for an open-air theatre or a closed theatre, and I hope the ladies will agree with me that I have made it possible for quite a number of persons beautifully dressed to be seen at the same time. I can picture them passing up this staircase first showing the left side of the dress, then showing the back, then showing the right side of the dress, then they could turn round, and we could see the front part, then we should see the back again, then we should see the left side again, and then they would disappear. And as they passed up the steps they would be placed against that which is only a little less beautiful than they are, some golden statue or statue in ivory by a master, and these little golden and ivory statues would mark the different stages of their progress as they ascended and descended, and finally, she who wished to look most beautiful of all would turn on arriving at the top of the staircase where two figures make an archway, a willing frame to beauty. Ladies, I am entirely at your service. If only those people with thousands of pounds, who do not know what to do with them, would put them at the service of art, we would have your theatre up for you in less than a year, and in that theatre,

ENTRANCE HALL OF A THEATRE                                    1906

# ENTRANCE HALL OF A THEATRE

before you passed into the performance where perhaps you too might derive some pleasure—you would be able to teach much to the clod-hoppers and the snobs, and those who go to the theatre to drink whisky and tread on people's toes, for you would have a reception-room in which you could show by your grace what it is to be the most beautiful nation in the world.

A STUDY FOR MOVEMENT                                    1906

# A STUDY FOR MOVEMENT

ONE can understand that people have something to do with movement, and that the moon has something to do with movement. What steps have to do with movement, except as the recipients of movers, is not as clear to me on one day as it is on another day, and here I feel inclined to speak right against these steps. The design has, I think, some feeling of movement in it, but when I come to think of the way some dancing school may probably plump a big flight of hard steps at the end of their room and make poor girls run up and down them, posing like the dreadful things we want to escape from, then I curse anything so material as steps in connection with movement, and regret that I ever made any record suggesting a connection between the two things.

CUPID AND PSYCHE 1906

# CUPID AND PSYCHE

HOW can I speak about Cupid or Psyche? There is only one man who ever spoke well in the English language about these two, and this is what he said, and it was what he said that made this design :

"In a certain city lived a king and queen who had three daughters exceeding fair. But the beauty of the two elder, though pleasant to behold, yet passed not the measure of human praise, while such was the loveliness of the youngest that men's speech was too poor to commend it worthily and could express it not at all. Many of the citizens and the strangers whom the fame of this excellent vision had gathered thither, confounded by that matchless beauty, could but kiss the finger-tips of their right hands at sight of her, as in adoration of the goddess Venus herself. And soon a rumour passed through the country that she whom the blue deep had borne, forbearing her divine dignity, was even then living among men, or that, by some fresh germination from the stars, not the sea now, but the earth, had put forth a new Venus, endued with the flower of virginity.

"This belief, with the fame of the maiden's loveliness, went daily farther into distant lands, so that many people were drawn together to behold that glorious model of the age. Men, sailed no longer to Paphos, to Cnidus, or Cythera, to the presence of the goddess Venus ; her sacred rites were neglected, her images stood uncrowned, the cold ashes were left to disfigure her forsaken altars. It was to a maiden that men's prayers were offered   .   .   ."

63

# MACBETH AND ROSMERSHOLM

THIS design and the one following I will take together. They are for two quite opposite types of drama, Shakespeare and Ibsen. The first is for the Sleep-walking Scene in "Macbeth," and the second for the room in the "Home of Rosmer." The first is for high classical tragedy, and the second for modern domestic drama. In each case the catastrophe is to a whole house, the houses of Macbeth and Rosmer, and in each case the author causes a woman to be the active creator of the catastrophe. But can anyone tell me how it is that the grandeur of Ibsen, his mystery and his force, are eclipsed by the greater mystery and force of Shakespeare? Judged by comparison with any modern author, Ibsen seems to me to be a giant, and then, judged by the side of Shakespeare, where does he disappear to? He disappears into his own particular little house, and Shakespeare is still sailing free over the mountains.

What, then, is the extraordinary difference between Shakespeare and Ibsen? A few centuries cannot be the explanation. I take it that it is this, that Shakespeare was an artist, and Ibsen is not—that Ibsen is an extraordinary man, and that he is one of the most extraordinary men of the nineteenth century, that he is solving the problems which other people cannot or will not solve, that he is putting questions which no other person ever puts, and that all the time he remains comparatively of no importance because he is not an artist. Ibsen somehow seems frightened of being commonplace, ordinary, what we call simple. And one feels this when one compares him to Shakespeare, a thing people tell us we should never do. But I am not so sure about that; in fact, I think it is very necessary and very good. Unless you fix a standard for dramatic literature and compare dramas with that standard, the world would be accepting the tenth-rate instead of the first-rate. And the first-rate is not Shakespeare, but Æschylus. But Æschylus refuses to enter a closed-in theatre, with its artificial light, and refuses to be entirely comprehensible to any but Greeks—to those Greeks who are dead.

64

MACBETH—SLEEP-WALKING SCENE

1906

ROSMERSHOLM

1906

# MACBETH AND ROSMERSHOLM

But this much we English can comprehend : it is that *our* highest standard of drama is that mingled literary and theatrical art which Shakespeare gave us as drama. Feeling this, I suppose, I have never yet dared to design a scene for Æschylus, although I have read his Trilogy Heaven knows how many times. They act them to-day in closed-in theatres, and they prance and gesticulate, and even venture phonetically to speak his lines in Greek. Why not let the old monument alone ? It stands there crumbling away ; better not to touch it, better to build up outside, taking it as a standard.

# A PALACE, A SLUM, AND A STAIRWAY

I DARESAY that, looking at these and several of the other designs, you may imagine that in their original form they are grey, but they are not. For instance, this is a design in blue, yellow, white, red, and black. I mention this because grey is rather depressing, and to depress is not my wish.

I was asked how I should design a scene containing suggestions of the dwellings of the upper and lower classes, and also put into the scene a neutral spot where the two classes always met. So I designed, on the one side, a palace, of which the only thing palatial about it was its upright and severe form, and its golden colour, and on the other side a slum, with its little windows and shadows, and its geranium in the window; and in between these two came a stairway, as the magic spot where the whole world meets practically in harmony. It is for no particular plot or play, but one can imagine that perhaps some day a writer or even a stage manager will perhaps plan a series of dramas dealing with these two classes, wherein we see them separated and then continually united. Who knows, I might do it with proper care myself if someone doesn't light-heartedly seize the idea carelessly and, slapping me on the back, tell me cheerily I'm good to steal from.

A PALACE, A SLUM, AND A STAIRWAY　　　　1907

SCREENS

1907

# SCREENS

"The Spectacle has, indeed, an emotional attraction of its own, but of all the parts, it is the least artistic, and connected least with the art of poetry. For the power of tragedy, we may be sure, is felt even apart from representation and actors. Besides, the production of spectacular effects depends more on the art of the stage machinist than on that of the poet."

ARISTOTLE's *Poetics*, VI. i. 19.

WHILE reading this, one must remember that Aristotle is a man who opens his discourse by stating that all art is Imitation. This is, of course, an exaggeration. It is so exaggerated that one might say that art has nothing whatever to do with Imitation. Just as he has exaggerated in that way, so does he exaggerate in this when he speaks of Spectacle. One can hardly say of Aristotle that he is a bad writer, but writers who wish to be held as great writers must be careful to choose the exact word.[1] Aristotle here wishes to speak about the scene in which tragedy or drama is represented. Why, then, does he use the word "spectacle"? Why, then, does he also go on to speak about spectacular effects? For this gives us the idea that he is talking about something common-place and vulgar, whereas we know that scene can be beautiful, not merely effective—beautiful. The remnants of the scene at Taormina are beautiful. I suppose that Aristotle is speaking of some degenerate form of spectacle, but why does he choose a bad example of scenic art when he wishes to compare it with the fine poetic art? Is it possible that Aristotle could be unfair? He almost runs it down. If he had spoken of spectacle as an enemy of the art of poetry, and of poetry as an enemy of the art of spectacle, he would have done better, but to put the art of poetry up on a high place and say that that vulgar fellow Spectacle has nothing whatever to do with so exalted a personage is both preposterous and ill-judged.

What all this has to do with the picture facing, I don't know; but as I have left out all the figures from the scene, and as nothing is happening there,

---

[1] Perhaps it is the translators of Aristotle who are to blame.

as no word is being spoken, I suppose I was feeling that I had removed spectacle or scene from the realms of poetry, thereby preventing any future contamination to the art of poetry.

I remember. Just as I was forgetting. Enemies will always make you forget friends for a moment.

My friend W. B. Yeats says that the scene is by no means disconnected with the art of poetry. What is to be done for the poor stage, when Aristotle threatens and Yeats beckons? Was there ever such a spectacle as this poor stage has presented for centuries? In fact I have passed through London and found no other woman so poor and so low as she is. And for that reason I intend to do all I can to place her higher than anyone else.

MACBETH, ACT I. SCENE 5        1908

# MACBETH

ACT I.—SCENE 6.

*Before the Castle ; hautboys ; servants of* MACBETH *attending.*

*Enter* DUNCAN, MALCOLM, DONALBAIN, BANQUO, LENNOX, MACDUFF, ROSS, ANGUS, *and* Attendants.

*DUNCAN.* This castle hath a pleasant seat ;
     The air nimbly and sweetly recommends itself
Unto our gentle senses.
     *Banquo.*                    This guest of summer,
The temple-haunting martlet, doth approve,
By his loved mansionry, that the heaven's breath
Smells wooingly here : no jutty, frieze,
Buttress, nor coign of vantage but this bird
Hath made his pendent bed and procreant cradle :
Where they most breed and haunt, I have observ'd
The air is delicate.

*Enter* LADY MACBETH.

     *Duncan.*            See, see, our honoured hostess !—
The love that follows us, sometime is our trouble,
Which still we thank as love.   Herein I teach you,
How you shall bid God 'ild us for your pains
And thank us for your trouble.
     *Lady Macbeth.*                All our service,
In every point twice done, and then done double,
Were poor and single business to contend
Against those honours deep and broad,

69

# MACBETH

Wherewith your majesty loads our house ;
For those of old, and the late dignities
Heap'd up to them, we rest your hermits.
    *Duncan.*                    Where's the Thane of Cawdor ?
We cours'd him at the heels, and had a purpose
To be his purveyor ; but he rides well,
And his great love (sharp as his spur), hath holp him
To his home before us.   Fair and noble hostess,
We are your guest to-night.
    *Lady Macbeth.*        Your servants ever
Have theirs, themselves, and what is theirs, in compt,
To make their audit at your highness' pleasure,
Still to return your own.
    *Duncan.*           Give me your hand ;
Conduct me to mine host ; we love him highly,
And shall continue our Graces towards him.
By your leave, Hostess.
                                  *[Exeunt.*

MACBETH, ACT II. SCENE 1                    1909

# MACBETH

ACT II.—SCENE 1

*MACBETH.* Go bid thy mistress, when my drink is ready,
She strike upon the bell.   Get thee to bed.

[*Exit* SERVANT.

Is this a dagger which I see before me,
The handle towards my hand ?   Come, let me clutch thee.
I have thee not, and yet I see thee still.
Art thou not, fatal vision, sensible
To feeling as to sight ? or art thou but
A dagger of the mind, a false creation,
Proceeding from the heat-oppressèd brain ?
I see thee yet, in form as palpable
As this which now I draw.
Thou marshall'st me the way that I was going ;
And such an instrument I was to use.
Mine eyes are made the fools o' the other senses,
Or else worth all the rest ; I see thee still ;
And on thy blade and dudgeon gouts of blood,
Which was not so before.—There's no such thing :
It is the bloody business, which informs
Thus to mine eyes.—Now o'er the one half world
Nature seems dead, and wicked dreams abuse
The curtain'd sleep ; witchcraft celebrates
Pale Hecate's offerings ; and wither'd murder,
Alarum'd by his sentinel, the wolf,
Whose howl's his watch, thus with his stealthy pace,

# MACBETH

With Tarquin's ravishing strides, towards his design
Moves like a ghost.—Thou sure and firm-set earth,
Hear not my steps, which way they walk, for fear
Thy very stones prate of my whereabout,
And take the present horror from the time,
Which now suits with it.   Whiles I threat, he lives;
Words to the heat of deeds too cold breath gives.

*(A bell rings.)*

I go, and it is done; the bell invites me.
Hear it not, Duncan, for it is a knell,
That summons thee to heaven, or to hell.                    [*Exit.*

MACBETH, Act II

1909

# MACBETH

IN his *Conversations with Eckermann*, Goethe once spoke as follows :
"In general, scenery ought to be of a tint favourable to the costumes which move before it, as the scenery of Beuther, which always tends more or less to dun colour, and lets the stuffs of the dresses stand out in all their freshness.

"If the scene painter is obliged to forsake this indefinite and very favourable tone, if it is necessary for him to paint a hall red or yellow, or a tent white, or a garden green, the actors ought in this case to take the precaution to avoid these colours in their costumes. If an actor in a red coat or green trousers walks across a red room, the upper part of his body disappears, and one only sees his legs; if he walks in the same costume in a green garden, it is his legs which disappear—only the upper part of his body remains. I have seen an actor in a white coat and very dark trousers who thus disappeared half way in standing against a white tent or dark background. And even when the scene painter represents a red or yellow room, or grass, he ought always to keep his tints rather low and aerial, so that the costumes can harmonise with them and produce their effect."

This is a lesson, this little lecture from Goethe, and should be learned thoroughly, and should be tested on the stage and the effect noted. Obviously one sees that it is a sensible thing to place a white costume against a dark background, and a dark costume against a light background. It makes the figure stand out; but what should you do when you want the figure to be merged in the scene, if not lost in the scene? Macbeth, roaming round his castle at night-time seems to be part of his habitation; and I remember that when Irving played the part he was dressed in a costume almost the same colour as the walls. Yet Irving went contrary to Goethe's advice, and Irving was right. But so was Goethe right. In fact there are many masters from whom you can learn, all of whom will be right, and all of whom will con-

73

tradict one another. This is a lesson to us not to be too cocksure, and the best thing to rely upon in such a case is your instinct, provided, at the same time, that you know everything that can be known. Knowledge cannot harm you, nor make your instinct less sharp. Knowledge is the very food for the instinct.

I wish I had more than crumbs to offer you on this table, but I cannot find stage scenery much better than dry bread at best.

MACBETH, ACT I. SCENE I                                    1909

# MACBETH

ACT I.—SCENE 1.

*An open place.   Thunder and lightning.*

*Enter three* WITCHES.

1 *WITCH.* When shall we three meet again
    In thunder, lightning, or in rain ?
2 *Witch.* When the hurlyburly's done,
When the battle's lost and won.
3 *Witch.* That will be ere the set of sun.
1 *Witch.* Where the place ?
2 *Witch.*                    Upon the heath.
3 *Witch.* There to meet with Macbeth.
1 *Witch.* I come, Graymalkin.
*All.* Paddock calls : anon !—
    Fair is foul, and foul is fair.
    Hover through the fog and filthy air.

                                  [WITCHES *vanish.*

MACBETH, ACT I. SCENE 1                    1909

# MACBETH

## ACT I.—SCENE 1.

ALTHOUGH this design and the one preceding it are for the same scene, and are practically the same idea, the two designs differ in certain particulars. When I showed the design to an actor-manager who shall be nameless,[1] he looked at it as if I had shown him a ghost, and he asked me what it was for. I told him that it was for the First Scene, First Act of "Macbeth," and that the three witches would be at the foot of the pillar, and so forth. I did not tell him that the straight pillar was to give the spectators the same feeling at the opening of the play as Beethoven gives his hearers in the opening of his Symphony Eroica. For he wanted something more matter-of-fact, and soon out it came. "Would you mind telling me," he said, "what that is supposed to represent?" Of course such a courteous question deserves a courteous answer, so I replied that my whole reason for placing the pillar there was that it should stand for the stone at Scone at which the Kings of Scotland were crowned. "Most interesting," he replied. Now had I been unable to furnish him with some historical fact to back up a purely fantastical, imaginative design made for a purely fantastical imaginative scene, he would have been dissatisfied. I am used to this sort of thing, and so I am generally ready with a stupid reply to a stupid question. But it would have been rather hard luck on a young man of twenty-one had this celebrated man plied him to give rhyme and reason to what was never intended to have rhyme or reason. To be quite fair to this actor-manager, I must say that he is not unique. There are quite a number of people like him, and one I came across in Berlin. You will see what this one asked me on page 30, when I was producing "Venice Preserved" in that city.

[1] Lest I shall be suspected of always meaning one celebrated actor-manager, I had better state here that I do not allude to Sir Herbert Beerbohm Tree.

"I go—and it is done: the bell invites me.— .Macbeth. Dedicated to Alexandre Dumas

MACBETH, ACT II

1910

# MACBETH

WHEN I exhibited this design at the Leicester Galleries a theatrical paper spoke of it as "a design, dedicated—ironically, we presume—to Alexandre Dumas *père*," and I have been wondering for a whole year how anybody could see irony in my dedication. This scene, although some stage might be discovered able to hold it—for if you look at the proportions, you will see that they are immense —is much more of a book illustration. Again, instead of being for high tragedy, it is for romance. It is not, in my mind, satisfactory for Shakespeare, and I thought it was just the thing that Alexandre Dumas would have liked. The bell is striking, and you hear it tinkling. The Romanticists of Dumas' period loved such things. Hernani's horn is just such another touch, not so Shakespearean as Romantic. The knocking at the door, *that* is Shakespearean.

> *Macbeth.*                              Whence is that knocking ?
> How is 't with me, when every noise appals me ?
> What hands are here ! Ha ! they pluck out mine eyes !
> Will all great Neptune's ocean wash this blood
> Clean from my hand ? No ; this my hand will rather
> The multitudinous seas incarnardine,
> Making the green—one red.

> *Re-enter* LADY MACBETH.

> *Lady Macbeth.* My hands are of your colour ; but I shame
> To wear a heart so white.—[*Knocking.*] I hear a knocking
> At the south entry :—retire we to our chamber :
> A little water clears us of this deed :
> How easy is it, then ! Your constancy
> Hath left you unattended.—[*Knocking.*] Hark ! more knocking :

79

# MACBETH

Get on your night-gown, lest occasion call us,
And show us to be watchers :—be not lost
So poorly in your thoughts.
    *Macbeth*. To know my deed, 'twere best not know myself.

                                              *[Knocking.*

Wake Duncan with thy knocking !  I would thou couldst !

                                              *[Exeunt.*

HAMLET, ACT I. SCENE 2                                                    1910

# HAMLET

THIS is the Second Scene, First Act of "Hamlet," as it was produced by me, with Mr. Stanislawsky's assistance, in the winter of 1911 at the Moscow Art Theatre.[1] You see the stage divided by a barrier. On the one side sits Hamlet, fallen, as it were, into a dream, on the other side you see his dream. You see it, as it were, through the mind's eye of Hamlet. That which is behind him is like molten gold. It is the Court of the King and Queen of Denmark. It is the grotesque caricature of a vile kind of royalty. The King speaks as if he were an automaton; his jaws snap on the words, he grunts them out ferociously. If you will read the words in the play, you will see that they are pure caricature, and should be treated as such. It is not an actual thing—it is a vision. The barrier which divides Hamlet from the Court is what you will, but to him it seems to be like the shrouded graves of his hopes, amongst which lies his father's body—murdered.

> *King.* Though yet of Hamlet our dear brother's death
> The memory be green, and that it us befitted
> To bear our hearts in grief, and our whole kingdom
> To be contracted in one brow of woe ;
> Yet so far hath discretion fought with nature
> That we with wisest sorrow think on him,
> Together with remembrance of ourselves.
> Therefore our sometime sister, now our queen,
> Th' imperial jointress to this warlike state,
> Have we, as 'twere with a defeated joy—
> With an auspicious and a dropping eye,
> With mirth in funeral, and with dirge in marriage,

[1] Sometimes called the Theatre of the Seagull.

81

# HAMLET

In equal scale weighing delight and dole—
Taken to wife : nor have we herein barr'd
Your better wisdoms, which have freely gone
With this affair along.   For all, our thanks.
Now follows, that you know, young Fortinbras,
Holding a weak supposal of our worth,
Or thinking by our late dear brother's death
Our state to be disjoint and out of frame,
Colleaguèd with this dream of his advantage—
He hath not fail'd to pester us with message,
Importing the surrender of those lands
Lost by his father, with all bonds of law,
To our most valiant brother.   So much for him.

HAMLET, Act II.

# HAMLET

A FEW years ago the attempt was made to employ curtains in place of scenery for the Elizabethan drama. The thought was a good one—but when it came to the further question of *how* to employ curtains in place of scenery, the thinkers gave it up ; that is to say, they contented themselves with " hanging up the clothes," with the result that the critics came along "and pecked off their nose."

The artist's ideas depend upon, and always appear simultaneously with, a fully-planned method for carrying his ideas out. The thinker's ideas are not so inspired. The artist's inspiration may fail, or it may wane like the moon—but while it lives it is an entirely complete and perfect power. It is for this reason that I attribute this idea of using curtains to the thinkers, and not to the artists.

When I began looking into the idea, I saw almost infinite possibilities in it, and for some time I developed the idea until it began to grow into a serious study. I shall return to it some day in my school and see whether or no it can yield all I want.

This design shows curtains of vast proportions and of great bulk. Perhaps you don't find it very clear. Yet my method for dealing with curtains is as clearly defined in my brain as the painting of a portrait is in the mind of a painter. Yet if you ask a painter to show you in a sketch what he intends to do, he will make a few marks here, a dash of colour there, and the scheme is complete. " Not for me," you say. But the scheme is not for you—the finished painting is.

Well, you shall have the finished work when I have dragged my materials from your million hands which cling to it like tentacles. You shall have the finished work when I have forced the fools who hinder everyone of us artists to realise, that they made a mistake to laugh at what they had not even the right to praise—to try and misunderstand what they have not even the power to forget.

We and you—we the artist, you the men and women who work—we have been and are still being swindled by the most damnable monster that ever finally found its way into a zoo. Its father was Lazyness, its mother Conceit, and it controls London, Paris, Berlin, and New York. It has no sense, no strength, no blood, no brain; yet it has a lot of money—and through this money it pretends to strength and sense, and too many women and men humour its pretensions.

I put woman first, for women could, and won't, settle the fate of this Earthworm.

Is there a single woman on earth who, reading this, will have the courage to release herself from the tyranny of the almighty and mighty weak power of the Dollar? Is there *one* woman out of all womankind who can and will put her power to the controlling of this amazing and tenth-rate monster?

"The Rhine gold, it was a true thing—no fable." So said a woman once to me. So feels many a woman to-day. Let them remember that there are other true things—and the truest is that the world looks to them to serve the cause of Beauty before the cause of votes; and that they have it in their power to do so, by destroying the brat Ugliness which is created solely by the ill-directed power of money.

So will they give new life to the whole world—to the whole world.

SCREENS—AS EMPLOYED FOR A LARGE STAGE SCENE

1912

# SCREENS

## SHOWING THEIR ARRANGEMENT FOR THE LAST ACT OF "HAMLET"

THE end of the book and the beginning of a new chapter in Scenography. I hope to see the day when the theatre will again become the theatre. At present it pretends to be the theatre, and therefore any pretender is welcome within the pasteboard citadel, and only pretence is estimated as genuine. The whole conspiracy is against art, against truth, and in favour of pretence.

Emotions are pretended, aped, not transformed by the magic of the artist into firm and beautiful shapes and patterns—into poems. Emotions are taken as they are, reflected in a mirror which is held rather low down—for the arms are getting tired—and this reflection we call art. This reflection is the merest pretence of art, and worse—it is a pretence and a parody of Life.

Life has become under the modern kind of tyranny a very little thing, easily pretended—put on and off like a pair of tennis shoes.

And the theatre is recording to-day for future ages, and for our children's children and their children, the facts of our infirmities—that our Imagination is sterile, and our Emotions tame ; that our hands are clumsy, and our voices faint.

Some to-day consider it their duty to comfort the age by assuring us that this is all as it should be, and that if the Imagination and Emotions of an age are weak, the art of the age must faithfully chronicle the fact for future ages. An amazing point of view. As if any eye can find time to linger Narcissus-like on the edge of destruction—wooing itself and its insipidities ; glorying in the silly reflection of a sillier reality.

The Imagination and the Emotions are not for purposes of mimicry—they are for creation. When the Imagination and the Emotions can, through art, create the age, how should they stoop to mimic it ? Art is useless after events : it must precede them—it must create them. When we elect a King, I think we do so with some art. When we celebrate his Coronation, I am sure we use no art at all.

# SCREENS

When we record that Coronation, our journalists have to bear the brunt. They are ordered to the front to fabricate by the use of false emotions and no Imagination, a true record of an event which was both childish and inadequate. Were Imagination ordered to the front, it would first of all create a coronation ceremony which would inspire even the King himself, and our records after the event would inspire the people.

When we build a city, art is not reckoned with. After the city is there, some records, photographic and caligraphic, are taken of it. These records serve but as a laughing-stock and a warning to future ages, recording the folly of blundering at the beginning, and taking infinite pains when it is too late : recording how through fear we omit to face facts about nations, cities, peoples, even our own lives, because it seems so costly—no other reason—and how we are forced in the end to pay a thousand times the price for what we could have had, had we but trusted our Imagination and our Emotions.

That the men of the theatre will realise this if none others will is my hope— and let them remember this : that their art, the art of the theatre, is perhaps the sole art which is still part of our life, and is not only deeply rooted in the heart of the people—its Imaginative, its universal heart is the people's heart.

" Popular " is a word which has lost its meaning—and to-day implies vulgarity, and that alone. But we are sure, are we not, that the true sense of the word " popular " implies an Ideal.

We are sure of this. Otherwise, had we not given up the game of Life, centuries ago ?

The Ideal, the popular Ideal of the theatre, should be to recreate a Life on a true stage, which might inspire the people to fresh endeavour. Preaching never did that, and never will. Only by Imagination and through the men of Imagination can such endeavour be awakened in the people.

The people know . . . there is no need to lie to them ; there is less reason to waste millions of money lying to ourselves. There are journals, large and mighty, lying daily to themselves. They tell themselves that they are mighty and that they are governing the people.

They are being fooled by the people—let them know it. If the people dislike tyranny of all kinds, how then shall they be fooled to like this cheap new tyranny ?

There is only one power which commands to-day, as it has always commanded

# SCREENS

in the past. It is the Imaginative Power. It is this which I call Royal. The Imaginative Power holds both the King and the People, the Rich and the Poor, in the same embrace—for these are its children. It holds them and regards them without preference—but is prejudiced always in the favour of Beauty. It punishes—it forgives; to be quite true, it always forgives—while punishing. It is the only good Power. Every man has a share of it—an equal share—and some families have held it more precious than gold, and others have sold it for a share in a mine. Those families to whom it is precious still predominate, and are bound together by the strongest and most lasting bonds that nature ever made or will make. Long live this King of Kings.

# AFTERWORD

THE popularisation of Ugliness, the bearing of false witness against Beauty— these are the achievements of the Realistic Theatre. I wish these Designs of mine to stand as my protest against the Realistic Theatre and its anarchistic tendency.

The modern Realistic Theatre, forgetful of all the Laws of Art, sets out to reflect the times. It reflects a small particle of the times, it drags back a curtain and exposes to our view an agitated caricature of Man and his Life, a figure gross in its attitude and hideous to look upon.

This is true neither to life nor to art. It has never been the purpose of art to reflect and make uglier the ugliness of things, but to transform and make the already beautiful more beautiful, and, in following this purpose, art shields us with sweet influences from the dark sorrows of our weakness.

The modern Realistic Theatre helps to stir up in the people that restlessness which is the enemy of all things.

The duty of the Theatre (both as Art and as an Institution) is to awaken more calmness and more wisdom in mankind by the inspiration exhaling from its beauty.

Photographic and Phonographic Realism injure the minds of the people. They thrust upon them a grotesque and inaccurate representation of the outward and visible life—with the divine essence—the spirit—the beauty of life left out.

Unimportant is it what subject the artist turns to—his pleasure is to illumine all that he touches so that it shall shine brightly. A momentary glance at the works of the Masters will endorse the truth of the statement.

But this modern Realistic Theatre pays no heed to the Masters, even if it be aware of the existence of their works.

Realism contains the seeds of Revolt, and however much the heart of man may lean with pity towards those whom fate seems to follow relentlessly,

# AFTERWORD

the artist must never lend his art, with its terrible power of appeal, towards the destruction of that just Balance which it is the aim of mankind to create and preserve. For there is no poison more swift than that which eats into the mind—this false-witnessing Realism—this traitor to the Imagination—this idolatry of ugliness to which the Realistic Theatre would compel us.

This thing first appeared in Paris, but only after 1789! For a time it flourished, but, while exciting the mob it revolted the intelligent.

Then it passed into Russia, into Germany, into Portugal and other restless places.

Neither in England nor America, nor yet in Ireland has it ventured—in these lands the Theatre often succeeds in its vulgarities without the aid of Realism.

Daring and dangerous—it is a Revolt against the very Laws of the Art of the Theatre.

Daring, because to *reproduce* nature is an impossibility.

Dangerous, because it is a threat against the well-ordered life of the Citizen. Each whisper of Revolt finds an echo in the Theatre of Realism—the gloomy expressions, the shuffling movements—the dark and closed-in scenes—the spasmodic exclamations of the actors—the strange muffled atmosphere—all these things lend themselves to form one sinister impression.

Alas! all this is false and unworthy of the theatre, both as an institution of the realm and as an Art.

With the Freedom of the theatre—free to select *what* it shall show—free from the tutorship of the other arts as to *how* it shall show—comes new hope.

Only by its freedom can its health be restored.